All About Plants

All About
Leaves

Claire Throp

Raintree

Raintree is an imprint of Capstone Global Library Limited, a company incorporated in England and Wales having its registered office at 7 Pilgrim Street, London, EC4V 6LB – Registered company number: 6695582

www.raintreepublishers.co.uk
myorders@raintreepublishers.co.uk

Text © Capstone Global Library Limited 2015
First published in hardback in 2014
The moral rights of the proprietor have been asserted.

Edited by Claire Throp and Brynn Baker
Designed by Peggie Carley
Picture research by Ruth Blair
Production by Victoria Fitzgerald
Originated by Capstone Global Library Ltd
Printed and bound in China by RR Donnelley Asia

ISBN 978 1 406 28438 6
18 17 16 15 14
10 9 8 7 6 5 4 3 2 1

British Library Cataloguing in Publication Data
A full catalogue record for this book is available from the British Library.

Acknowledgements
We would like to thank the following for permission to reproduce photographs: Dreamstime: Egon Zitter, 7, Mommamoon, 16, Erin Packard Photography, 21; iStock: Tedy2g, 12; Shutterstock: Barry Blackburn, 14, Bobkeenan Photography, 17, byggarn.se, 18, Chris Bence, 20, DenisNata, 9, 23 (middle), Elena Elisseeva, 4, Filipe B. Varela, 5, Nataliya Hora, 10, Pefkos, cover, Photobac, 22, pixelman, 13, 23 (bottom), Smileus, 6, 11, Songquan Deng, back cover, 19, 23 (top), Suphatthra China, 15, Triff, 8.

We would like to thank Michael Bright for his invaluable help in the preparation of this book.

Every effort has been made to contact copyright holders of material reproduced in this book. Any omissions will be rectified in subsequent printings if notice is given to the publisher.

Contents

What are plants?

Plants are living things.

flower

stem

leaf

root

seed

Plants have many parts.

What do plants need to grow?

Plants need sunlight and air to grow.

Plants need water to grow.

What are leaves?

A leaf is one part of a plant.

Leaves grow from a plant's **stem**.

Leaves make food for the plant.

Leaves use sunlight to make the food.

Types of leaves

There are different types of leaves. Some leaves are long and thin.

Some leaves have **wavy** edges.

Some plants have very big leaves.

Some plants have very
small leaves.

Colours

Most leaves are green.

Some leaves stay green all year.

Some leaves turn red in autumn.

Other leaves turn yellow, orange, or brown in autumn.

Leaves as food

Some animals like to eat leaves.

Some insects like to eat leaves too.

Plants need leaves

Leaves make food to help a plant grow.

Picture glossary

 **autumn** season when leaves turn red, yellow, orange, and brown

 **stem** strong part of a plant that holds up the leaves

 **wavy** many curves in a line

Index

Notes for parents and teachers

Before reading

Gather together a variety of leaves or photos of leaves. If it is not autumn, find photos of leaves before and after they have changed colour. Ask children why they think some leaves change colour and some do not. Talk about how some leaves change during different seasons.

After reading

- Ask children why leaves are so important for plants. (They make food.)

- If possible, take the children outside and see if they can find a selection of different shaped leaves. Then use books or the internet to work out the type of plants or trees.

- Work with children to capture ideas about leaves, such as descriptions of their colours, why leaves are useful, and so on. Ask them to use vivid adjectives and precise verbs, such as *scarlet shapes against the branches* or *food and shelter for other living things.* After the children have contributed phrases, work as a class to combine those phrases to create a poem. Children may add illustrations or photos to the class poem.